BACK IN THE DAY

Reflections of a Baby Boomer Childhood

FRED BARNETTE

NEWMAN SPRINGS PUBLISHING
320 Broad Street
Red Bank, NJ 07701

First originally published by Newman Springs Publishing 2023

ISBN 979-8-88763-930-7 (Paperback)
ISBN 979-8-88763-931-4 (Digital)

Printed in the United States of America

To my parents:
Fred L. Barnette, 1924–2005
Wilmith Barnette, 1924–2020

Foreword

I have always been interested in previous generations. My grandmother told me about pie socials held during her youth. Girls would bake pies, and guys could bid on them. If you had the highest bid, you had the opportunity to sit down and meet the girl. My relatives are from West Virginia. My grandmother also taught me how to clog. Clogging is a mountain folk dance. It was fascinating to hear my mother describe living in a coal mine town. My dad would tell me about being drafted right out of high school and fighting in the Battle of the Bulge. They were members of "the greatest generation."

I enjoy watching historical movies. Hearing the music, seeing the fashion, noticing cars they drove is always interesting. In *Back to the Future*, we return to the fifties. The movie *The Help* shows life in the sixties. *Forrest Gump* takes us through the baby boomer years of the fifties, sixties, and seventies.

I am a member of the baby boomer generation. We are members who were born between 1946 and 1964. This book will describe our childhood and adolescence experiences. I have verbally told people some of my childhood adventures. People often say, "You should write a book."

So I decided to do just that. Sit back and enjoy reading about the fifties and sixties. Time passes so quickly. It seems like yesterday.

Contents

The Ring

It was an exciting day in March of 1967. I had been anticipating the arrival of my class ring. Class rings were important to students back in 1967. There was a thing called "going steady" between a girl and boy. Now they call it "in a relationship." If a guy decided he wanted to go steady with a girl, he would ask her. If she said, "Yes," then he would give her his class ring. The ring was always too big for the girl's finger. Somehow, girls would melt wax inside the ring band so it would fit. When you broke up (and most of them did), the girl would just give the ring back.

Class rings are outdated now. I am not sure they even make them anymore. I am seventy-two now and have four grown-up sons—thirty-one, thirty-three, forty, and forty-two. None of them ever mentioned a desire to own a class ring. They were especially important to the baby boomer generation, though.

Well, I had the ring now, but no sign of a girlfriend. That would all change in five months. She came out of nowhere.

Varsity Letter Jacket

Another important item was the varsity letter jacket. I just had to have one of those. Your self-esteem was zero unless you earned that varsity letter. The summer before my first year, I was notified that the band teacher wanted all incoming members to report to the high school parking lot. All first-year students needed a crash course on football field marching. There I was, marching around the parking lot with a bunch of girls holding their flutes and clarinets. From the parking lot, you could look down on the football field and see the players practicing. I should be down there. I just had one problem. I was six feet tall, and I only weighed 136 pounds. Track was my ticket for a varsity letter.

In 1967, you had to earn at least fifteen points to receive a varsity letter. First place was five points, second place was three points, and third place was worth one point. The coach asked me to run the two-mile race. That is eight times around a track. We had no two milers. I was not crazy about it either. Who really wants to run around a track eight times?

Distance runners must train year-round to be effective. In the fall, they compete in cross-country. My school did not have a cross-country team because they could not find a coach. In the winter, they ran indoor track. In the spring, they ran outdoor track. I had two weeks to train for the first track meet against archrival Richard Montgomery High.

The big day came, and we traveled to Richard Montgomery for the first track meet. One of my teammates overheard several Richard Montgomery runners talking. They said, "Gaithersburg only has one two-miler, and he isn't very good."

I was determined to prove them wrong. I went out fast and led after six laps. The lack of training hurt me down the stretch, and two runners passed me. I did get third and one point toward that varsity letter. I had fourteen more points to go. The track season ended, and I had only earned fourteen points. The awards assembly for spring sports would be in two weeks. Track team members came up to me at various times and asked, "Do you think Coach will still give you a letter, even though you're one point short?"

I truly had no idea. I was graduating in June, and it was my last shot at a varsity letter. The day of the awards assembly for spring sports arrived. I listened to all the names of the varsity letter winners. Then I heard it, "Two miler Fred Barnette." What a thrill it was. I needed to get that jacket and have the letter sewn on. It was June, and a little warm for a letter jacket. Mornings could be cold, riding a motorcycle to school, so it got plenty of use. The letter is hanging in my garage. It still brings back memories of the '68 season and the coach that decided to let one point slide.

Today, the fifteen-point minimum requirement is gone. There is a track and cross-country program for girls. In 1967, girls only had two choices for sports. They could play tennis or participate in field hockey. Varsity letter jackets are no longer cool. My four sons all earned varsity letters, but none of them wore a jacket. My oldest son earned a varsity letter in football, baseball, and track. I bought him a jacket, but he never wore it.

Varsity letter jacket

Wheels

I got a class ring and a letter jacket. What else do you need in high school?

Students older than sixteen had to have some type of wheels. You could borrow the family car, but how would you get to school each day? It was so uncool to ride a school bus in your junior and senior years. When I was fourteen, I bought a motorbike from a hardware store. You would start off by pedaling, and then a small motor would start. It could go about twenty-five miles per hour. My neighborhood friends called it toy toot. There was one problem with the motorbike. You could not get a license plate for it. It was a lot of fun in the neighborhood, but you could not ride it on the highway.

When I turned sixteen, I decided to get a real motorcycle. I needed a cosigner to finance the motorcycle. My father refused to cosign because they were too dangerous. I discussed the cosigning problem with my thirteen-year-old brother. We knew my father was an impulse buyer. We just needed to get him to the showroom floor. We talked my father into at least going to the Yamaha dealer and looking at the motorcycles. We showed up at the dealership, and he saw all the brand-new, shiny Yamaha and BSA motorcycles. Dad looked them over and said, "Oh, I see why you boys like these motor-cycles." He cosigned, and I became the owner of a brand-new, red Yamaha Twin Jet 100.

I rode that motorcycle everywhere, year-round, and in any kind of weather. I rode it to school and work. It was a chick magnet. Lots of girls asked to ride on it. There was always one problem. I never had an extra helmet with me. I received several traffic tickets for no passenger helmet. I also got traffic tickets for passing other vehicles without changing lanes.

If traffic was stopped on a two-way highway, I would go between the two rows of cars. Eventually, my license was revoked for sixty days. Hitchhiking was my new form of transportation during the suspension.

One day, a beautiful girl named Wendy asked me if I could give her a ride to Georgetown on the motorcycle. Georgetown was a cool place to hang out. Georgetown University is located there. It is a section of Washington, DC. It was a long trip, at least an hour away. She was so beautiful I had to say yes. Could this be my first girlfriend? I thought I had a chance. It was a beautiful, warm summer day. I had visions of walking up and down the street, window-shopping. I could try holding her hand. My dream immediately crashed. She got off the motorcycle and ran across the street without saying anything. She fell into the arms of some other guy. Are you kidding me? I gave her a ride all the way to Georgetown so she could see her boyfriend. She never said a word to me. She never even said, "Thank you."

I should have asked a few questions before we left Gaithersburg. Chalk this one up to experience.

Yamaha Twin Jet 100

Baby Boomer Electronic Games

The baby boomer generation only had one electronic game. It was called electronic football. The players were little plastic figures that you placed on a vibrating football field. There was an on-off switch. After you set up the players, you turned the switch on, causing the field to vibrate. The players would start moving. If a defensive player touched the running back, the play was over. Now you had to physically arrange all the players on the board for the next play. Sometimes, the running back would head off in the wrong direction. You had to turn the board off and turn him around. Pass plays were next to impossible. You would place a little felt ball in the quarterback's hand. The hand went forward, causing the felt football to fly. If it hit a receiver, it was complete. We would play electronic football for hours. I still see electronic football games at yard sales or antique stores. That was it for electronic games.

Slide football was also popular among baby boomers. The football was made from a single sheet of paper. Kids would fold the paper up into a small triangle. Two players would sit down across from each other at a table. They would use the width of the table. One player would place the football on the edge of the table and hit it with the palm of his hand. The football would slide across the table. Next, he would turn the palm of his hand up. The player would strike the football a second time with his index finger. The object was to get the football to stop on the edge of the table. If the football was short of the edge or slid off the table, their turn was over. If the football stayed on the edge, a player would place their index finger under the football and flick it in the air. If you caught the football in the air, you scored a touchdown. Kicking the extra point was always fun. The opponent would form a pistol with both hands. They touched each pistol by the barrel (the two index fingers). Your thumbs pointed straight up, forming the goalpost.

The football was placed on the table by one of its points. This caused the longest side of the football facing the kicker. The kicker would flick the football with their index finger. If the football went between the thumbs, the extra point was successful. We played slide football before school and at lunch. We also played it at home. I don't see slide football being played anymore. Baby boomers had a blast with it. I make paper footballs occasionally now. Sometimes, I make a paper football out of gum wrappers.

Baby boomers lived in the street. Pickup football games were very popular. We played touch if you were in the street and tackle if you were on the grass. Occasionally, we would take our neighborhood team and go play a team from another neighborhood. That game was always tackle with no equipment. Nobody ever got hurt. Parents would sometimes officiate. The prettiest girl in the neighborhood would ride her bike by the football game in our neighborhood. I always wanted to have some spectacular play as she rode by. I should have quit the game and run home to get my bike. I have noticed pickup football games now. It seems to be a rare occurrence.

Today baseball, football, and basketball games are played in organized youth athletic associations.

Touch on the street, tackle on the grass

There was a popular game that girls played called "Jacks." The girl would hold ten little metal objects called jacks in the palm of her hand. She would toss the jacks on the floor, about four inches off the ground. The ball was dropped from about waist-high from a sitting position. The girl would pick up one jack and then catch the ball. She would do this for each jack until she collected all ten. Next, she would try to collect two jacks before catching the ball. She would then attempt picking up three, four, five six, seven, eight, nine, and finally, all ten. If she missed, her opponent would take a turn. My sister played Jacks every day. She was unbeatable. I think Jacks disappeared sometime in the sixties. Nobody plays Jacks anymore.

Dodgeball games have stood the test of time until recently. Some school districts have outlawed dodgeball. Students would have a legal way of picking on an unpopular student whom most students despised. I am a retired assistant principal at a middle school. I witnessed it firsthand.

In the fifth grade, during recess, we were playing dodgeball outside. A little field mouse ran across the blacktop through our game. Several boys pounced on the mouse to catch it. It vanished in thin air. The mouse just disappeared. We were in line, waiting to reenter the building. I felt something moving in my pants. I pulled the mouse out of my pants, inside the classroom. It must have run up my pant leg. The teacher told me to take the mouse outside. On my fifth-grade report card, there was a section called "Comments." The teacher wrote, "We really got a kick out of Fred pulling a mouse out of his pants after recess."

The Accident

Teenage car accidents were a problem for the baby boomer generation. They continue to be a problem today. Everybody can name several classmates that have been in serious car accidents. In fact, most people know students who lost their lives.

I had a near-death experience myself. It was April 1967. I was driving home from track practice. It was raining. I was thinking about the dilemma my neighbor was in. His parents went on vacation, and he took the car out. He was in a car accident. He was not injured, but the car was totaled. They would be arriving home today. Thirty seconds later, I was in my own car accident. In 1967, seatbelts only consisted of a lap belt. Unfortunately, I wasn't wearing mine. I was crossing a bridge that had a slight turn in it. The car skidded off the road and hit the guardrail. It would have been a minor fender bender if I was wearing a seatbelt.

The impact caused me to slide across the seat and land on the passenger-side floor. The car took a ninety-degree turn and crossed the road. I could tell I was airborne. The car was facing up and then took an immediate turn down. I could see tree limbs hitting the windshield. The nose of the car ended up in the creek. The back of the car was caught on the guardrail. It was hanging by the trailer hitch. The 1964 Pontiac Tempest was a convertible. If the car flipped, I would have been crushed or drowned.

I was unhurt, except the outside of my ear was bleeding. I waded through the creek and climbed the bank. I crossed the street and went to a house. I explained what happened and asked to use the phone. I called my father and told him I was involved in an accident at the bridge. He wanted to know how bad it was. I felt uncomfortable being in this strange house, so I just said it was minor. My father came down with my little brother in the car. He couldn't believe his eyes when he rounded a bend in the road and saw his car hanging off the bridge. I'll never forget the words he said to me, "My god, boy, you ruined me!" He had just made his last car payment. I was so lucky to still be alive.

The bridge

Music

Baby boomers saw a dramatic change in music. We saw the end of the big band swing era and the birth of rock and roll. My father loved the big bands. He played trumpet in several successful working dance bands. He always blamed poor Elvis Presley for ending the big band swing era. My father said, "That old Elvis, he finally shook himself to death."

There were several performers that introduced this new style of music. You had Buddy Holly, Little Richard, Deon and the Belmont's, Chuck Berry, Jerry Lee Lewis, Fats Domino, and Bill Haley and the Comets, to name a few. Girl groups also popped up overnight. Popular girl groups were The Ronettes ("Be My Baby"), The Shirelles ("Will You Still Love Tomorrow"), Martha Reeves and the Vandellas ("Dancing in the Street"). Who could forget later groups like The Supremes ("Stop in the Name of Love) and Gladys Knight and the Pips ("Midnight Train to Georgia")?

I used to spy on my sister when she had friends over in the basement around 1962. They were learning all the new dances. You could hear Dee Dee Sharp singing "Mashed Potato Time," Little Eva doing "The Locomotion," or The Orlans singing "The Wah Watusi." I must admit, I had a crush on Barbie, one of her friends. There was a guy named Ernest Evans from Philadelphia that started a dance craze. His stage name was Chubby Checker, and he taught all of us a new dance called "The Twist." Chubby had a great follow-up hit called "Let's Twist Again."

Rock and roll took over by 1955, and the big band swing era was a thing of the past. I'm so sorry, Dad.

The British Invasion

I n 1960, four young men formed a band in Liverpool, England. Their names were John, Paul, George, and Ringo. The name of the band was the Beatles.

In 1964, their plane landed in New York City. They took America by storm. Kids were absolutely crazy about them. I was in eighth grade in 1964, and I was invited to a party. It was held outside at night. The Beatles album was playing on the record player. A kid wanted to read the name of the album as it was playing. He held a candle close to the record to read the label. Candle wax dripped down on the album. You would have thought World War III had started. I thought somebody was going to kill him. All the girls loved the Beatles' long hair, clothes, and British accents. American guys started wearing their hair longer. There was not much we could do about the British accents.

America was invaded by other British groups. The Rolling Stones had a huge following. In 1965, they released a song called "Satisfaction." It was the number one song for six weeks. Other British groups included Herman's Hermits, Dave Clark Five, The Buckinghams, The Who, The Yardbirds, The Zombies, The Animals, Jerry and the Pacemakers, The Hollies, Chad and Jeremy, Peter and Gordon, and Manfred Man. Two British ladies also had successful careers. In 1965, Petula Clark had a monster hit called "Downtown." The following year, Dusty Springfield had a number one hit called "You Don't Have to Say You Love Me." Eventually, the British groups gradually started to fade because something called Motown came on the scene.

Motown

The baby boomers saw the end of big band swing music and the birth of rock and roll. We were invaded by the British music groups. There was one more genre in music that occurred before we left childhood and became young adults. James Brown released a song called "I Feel Good" in 1964. It was a new sound that made you want to get out there on the dance floor. James Brown would slide across the floor on one leg, do twirls, drop the mic stand and catch it inches from the floor, and do splits. He worked himself up into a frenzy. Someone came from offstage and placed a cape over his shoulder and attempted to lead him offstage. James would walk to the edge of the curtain and then throw the cape off his shoulders and slide back out to the middle of the stage. He called it funk music.

Other Black artists followed James Brown's style and the term *soul music* was coined. The recordings were done in Detroit, under the direction of Barry Gordy. The music then became known as Motown music. The artists were exclusively Black. It was the best music for dancing. You couldn't stay in your seat. There was another big difference when you heard Motown music. They had a horn section. Trumpets, trombones, and saxophones were used. Suddenly, horn players were in demand.

Local Bands

I got a call from a popular group from a nearby town called Damascus in Maryland. They wanted to add horns to their band. My best friend, John, played sax, and I played trumpet. We would be billed soul brother number one and soul brother number two. The band was called "The Reverbs." They played parties, school dances, and teen centers. However, they were not committed to switching over to exclusive Motown music. They used the horns in only one set. It wasn't cost-effective adding two more musicians, so they dropped us. That was no problem. Most bands switched over to soul music, even though it meant extra band members.

John and I joined a brand-new start-up band. They were out of Gaithersburg, Maryland, our hometown. The leader of the band was named Charlie, and the band was called the "Stimulations." We learned three songs, and Charlie got us our first job playing a Methodist Youth Fellowship dance at Epworth United Methodist Church. I told Charlie we weren't ready because you had to have about forty songs to do a dance. It was a total disaster. We played our three songs: "Louie, Louie," "California Sun," and "The House of the Rising Sun." Kids seemed to like us, and we played all three songs again.

After hearing the songs twice, an adult chaperone approached Charlie and explained that the kids wanted to put on their records. Charlie refused, telling the man we took the job for free, and we were going to continue. We played the three songs again. The same adult approached the band a second time. He said, "Charlie, the kids have taken up a collection and will give it to you if you'll stop playing." I can't remember if Charlie took the money or not. We packed up our equipment and started to walk across the room. Some boy came up to Charlie and said, "Boy, you really suck!" Charlie chased him out of the building and smacked him around in the parking lot. In the history of music, this may never have happened to any other group. I never heard of a band being paid not to play.

In the sixties, there were no disc jockeys. Schools had dances every other week. Teen centers and church youth groups often scheduled dances. There were always lots of parties for which to play. The "Stimulations" learned their forty songs and played all those venues.

I got an audition offer for another working band. They were called "Perry Gray and the Other Side." Perry Gray was the lead singer. This band had an agent and some nice bookings. I went to the audition and got the job. We played some exclusive nightclubs in Washington, DC. My favorite was "Blackies House of Beef." It was an exclusive restaurant with a large party room. The song of the year in 1969 was "Raindrops Keep Falling on My Head," recorded by B. J. Thomas. It was used in the movie *Butch Cassidy and the Sundance Kid* and won the Academy Award for Best Song. Perry hated the song and wanted no parts of singing it. I gave it a shot and was selected to sing it. I remember playing a lot of private high school dances in Washington, DC, Maryland, and Virginia.

We got a dream booking in Ocean City, Maryland, for one week. There was a dance building right on the boardwalk. It was called the "Pier Ballroom." There was an arcade right across from the ballroom on the boardwalk. Above the arcade were four rooms. Bands performing in the Pier Ballroom stayed in those rooms for free. I was twenty years old and playing right on the boardwalk, every night for a week! The beach and ocean were right next to the Pier Ballroom. What a dream job! The keyboard player talked to some girl during a break on the first night.

The following night, she brought a friend with her. I talked to the friend on breaks during the second night. The friend's name was Michelle. Her parents owned a popular restaurant on nearby Fenwick Island, Delaware. It had huge polka dots painted on the outside of the building. Michelle just graduated from high school and would be attending the University of Delaware in the fall. She told me the band Chicago played at her prom when she was a junior. I didn't believe her. (Really? Chicago?) She told me one of their albums listed all their jobs for that year on the album cover. I checked, and, sure enough, her high school was listed on the album.

Michelle came every night to the band job. We spent time on the beach and boardwalk during the day. I heard "Summer Nights" from the musical *Grease*. The lyrics describe exactly what happened to me that week. I had a blast and met a girl crazy for me, she was cute as can be, and we splashed around in the ocean. I was in love by the time the week ended. In 1970, there were no cell phones, texting, or FaceTime. She never mentioned anything about staying at her house if I returned. We wrote a few old-fashioned letters. I couldn't afford motel prices. I drove a little unreliable sports car called a Triumph Spitfire. It would be an eight-hour car trip to see her. It just didn't work out, and she gradually became a distant memory.

Pier Ballroom is now *Ripley's Believe It or Not!*

Music: Ed Sullivan, "45s," Transistor Radios, American Bandstand, Malt Shops

The baby boomers listened to music all the time. There was no satellite Sirius radio, compact disc, 8-track tapes, cassette tapes, boom boxes, or internet. How did baby boomers listen to their favorite songs? Most of us had a small radio that fit in the palm of our hand. It was called a transistor radio. I think the radio only had an AM band. We would tune in to our favorite station. Mine was WINX 1600 out of Rockville, Maryland. The station would play the current top forty most popular songs. If we heard a song we loved, we would head to the nearest five- and ten-cent store. They sold 45 rpm records for about one dollar. The record would have just the song you loved on one side. There was another song on the flip side. The flip side song wasn't usually very good. I bought my records from the Ben Franklin five- and ten-cent store in Gaithersburg, Maryland. I don't think Ben Franklin stores exist anymore.

Students would walk to a favorite malt shop after school. They would listen to music from the jukebox. They usually ordered french fries with either a cherry or vanilla Coke. Students only stayed about an hour and then headed home.

American Bandstand would be on television when they got home. The host was Dick Clark. We would watch all the kids dance to the popular songs of the day. He would have three teenagers rate a new song and give their input on the song. Occasionally, there would be dance contests. The highlight of the show was a live performance from a current recording artist. The artist would lip-synch their current hit. Two performances have stayed with me through the years. Paul Revere and the Raiders recorded a number one song called "Kicks" in 1966. They came on *American Bandstand* dressed in Revolutionary War outfits. Gene Chandler had a smash hit called "The Duke of Earl" in 1961. He came down the aisle and onto the stage, wearing all black: top hat, tuxedo, and holding a cane. I was eleven, but I thought that was so cool. I also loved the song.

The goal of every recording artist was to be invited to perform on the Ed Sullivan television show. The show ran from 1948 to 1971. It was part of American television entertainment for twenty-three years. Only the biggest stars of the day got an invitation. It was a variety show with many forms of entertainment. The rock and roll performance was saved for last. In the sixties, some of the rock groups were censored. Elvis Presley could only be filmed from the waist up. The Rolling Stones had to change their lyrics from "Let's spend the night together" to "Let's spend some time together."

That pretty much took us through our baby boomer music years. In 1972, I was riding in my car with a friend. We saw a line several blocks long. What could cause all the excitement? The front of the line stopped in front of a movie theater. The pavilion advertised a movie called *Saturday Night Fever* starring John Travolta. It was the beginning of the next music craze. Disco music was born.

My childhood was over. I was twenty-two.

Transistor radio

Fire

A friend called me on the telephone during the summer of 1966. His name was Gary. He had to take his little brother Robbie to the barbershop for a haircut. He asked if I wanted to ride along. I said, "Sure, why not?"

We were going to Olney, Maryland, about twenty minutes away by car. I rode up front in the passenger seat. This is commonly known as riding shotgun. It was hot, so we had all the windows down. I was smoking a cigarette. I can't remember where I got it or why I was smoking it. I suppose most teenagers experiment with cigarettes a time or two. I tossed the cigarette butt out the window when I was finished. Twenty minutes later, we arrived at the barbershop. The shop was located above a drugstore. You had to climb some steep stairs to get to the shop. We waited about fifteen minutes before it was Robbie's turn. Halfway through Robbie's haircut, a man came charging into the room. He asked, "Does anybody own a green Buick LeSabre?" Gary stated that the car belonged to him. The man said, "Well, it's on fire!"

We ran down the stairs and out into the parking lot. A bus driver took a fire extinguisher off his bus and was putting the fire out. He got the fire out, but it left a hole in the back seat, about the size of a basketball. I felt terrible. The cigarette butt had blown into the back seat, causing the fire. Gary did not tell his father what happened. He simply put a gym bag over the hole. Things were fine for about two weeks. However, one day, Gary's father went to the grocery store. He was putting groceries in the back seat and had to move the gym bag. Gary had some explaining to do.

The Great Outdoors

I spent most of my childhood in the woods and fields surrounding my neighborhood. Most of the time, I was alone. I have always been a nature lover. I loved hiking down old logging trails or finding wild raspberries and blackberries. Creeks provided all kinds of adventures. I would flip over rocks in the creek and catch crayfish. The creeks had brightly colored minnows. Box turtles were everywhere back in the sixties. I could find one in the woods almost every day. The woods and fields provided a relaxing, quiet time. I would leave the house in the morning and spend all day there.

Box turtle

One day, I was feasting on wild raspberries when I heard a scratching noise. It was coming from underneath the bush. I bent down and discovered a baby box turtle. He was only the size of a silver dollar. Another time, I was walking down an old logging trail. Suddenly, I was surrounded by foxhounds. There must have been fifty of them. I decided to try to catch one and take it home. They were so occupied with the hunt they never stood still long enough for me to catch one. Then I saw men on horses with red jackets. I decided to abandon the idea and disappear.

Sometimes, I went into the woods with friends. On one occasion, we captured a blacksnake. We were walking home with it, trying to decide what to do. Somebody came up with the idea of putting it in a mailbox. So that's exactly what we did. We got back to the neighborhood and sat around, laughing about the snake. Can you imagine opening up your mailbox and seeing a blacksnake?

Gary didn't think it was so funny. He started panicking about it being a federal offense and the FBI getting involved. He really got all worked up. Another time, a group of junior high kids went down to the creek. An old dead tree had fallen over the creek, and we all climbed out on it. I have no idea how the topic came up, but we started talking about how girls get pregnant and have children. We had some wild theories, but none of us had a clue.

I had a favorite pond I visited at least once a week. It was a farm pond that bordered the woods. There was a high fence around the pond. No trespassing signs were not posted, but I knew the farmer did not want us there. He would occasionally ride his tractor down to the pond and chase us out. We could hear him coming. We brought in our fishing lines, hopped back over the fence, and disappeared into the woods. Several unusual and tragic events occurred at that farm pond.

One day, I went to the pond, and there was a pony inside the fence. I was probably about twelve. The pony seemed friendly enough, so I decided to try to ride him. He was right next to the fence. I climbed to the top of the fence and eased myself down on his back. He started spinning around, attempting to bite me. I spun off his back and hit the ground. I was not injured, but I wasn't going to try that again.

Finding bait was often a challenge for fishing. There was a huge tree at the edge of the pond. At the base of the tree, there were lots of loose soil perfect for earthworms. I started digging around there but didn't have any luck. I reached my hand further back in the tree trunk. I felt some kind of paper object deep within the trunk of the tree. I pulled it out. It was a letter in perfect condition. It was written in French. I had no idea what it said, but I took it home.

A college student lived across the street from my house. I went over to his house and showed him the letter. The student's name was Glen, and he attended the University of Virginia. Glenn knew enough French to figure out most of the letter. The letter was written by a girl to her boyfriend. She realized he probably would never find the letter. Apparently, her parents would not let her see him. I took the letter back to the tree and placed it back in the trunk. It might still be in the trunk of the tree to this day.

Another time, I decided to try fly-fishing at the pond. I stood on the bank and whipped the fly out on the water. I did this numerous times. A bat noticed this from a nearby tree and swooped down on the fly. The poor bat was caught by the wing. I brought him to shore and examined him. It was a little brown bat. Luckily, he was not injured, and the hook was easy to remove from his wing. A friend was at the pond with me. For some unknown reason, he brought a camera with him. He took a picture of me holding the bat up. I have the picture in my home office now. I show the picture to people who disbelieve the story.

On a cold winter day, three brothers and a neighborhood boy wandered down to the pond. The oldest boy, Billy, was ten. The other boys were in second or third grade. The ice was too thin, and all four boys broke through it. Billy was able to grab the neighborhood boy and get him to the shoreline. He went back into the pond to rescue his brothers. Sadly, Billy and his two brothers drowned. I never heard what the surviving boy did. I suppose he climbed the fence and ran home for help. He was only about seven. The mother and father moved out of the neighborhood after losing their three sons.

I soon got a reputation for my outdoor knowledge. My mother was making a dried flower arrangement for our living room. She wanted cattails added to the flowers. That was no problem. I knew a swampy area with plenty. A kindergarten teacher called my house.

She wanted her students to watch tadpoles become frogs. Someone told her to call me. I went to Griffith's Pond and found her plenty. A neighborhood child ran away from home. They thought he might be hiding somewhere in the woods. The police might need help finding some of the possible hiding locations. I was more than ready to help, but the police never came to my house. They found the boy hiding in a church.

Drive-In Movies

Baby boomers really enjoyed drive-in movie theaters. They were perfect for teenage dating. You could be alone and get passionate during the movie. They became known as the passion pit. You pulled your car into a big parking lot and located a speaker pole. The speaker would somehow fit into the driver's side window. The snack bar was in a separate building in the back to which you walked. The screen was huge. The last time I went to a drive-in movie was in 1973. It closed a few years later. There are no drive-in theaters where I live now. There are very few left in the nation.

In 1966, a few of my guy friends decided to go to the drive-in movies. I don't remember what was playing. We decided to hide two guys in the trunk for free admission. We opened the trunk up at my buddy's house. It was full of my dad's band stuff. His trumpet, stand, and all his music were in there. We took all of it out and hid the band equipment in the hedges. Everything went as planned. We got into the drive-in parking lot. When it was clear, the two guys in the trunk got out. The movie was playing when we heard an announcement from the public address system: "Will Fred Barnette please report to the snack bar?"

I wondered what on earth this could be about. When I got to the snack bar, I noticed my father in a panic. He told me that he had a band job, and all his equipment was in the trunk of the car (it's funny to think about now, but it wasn't funny then). I had to tell him the equipment was about thirty minutes away, hidden in some hedges. He never mentioned what happened after he left. I do know he went to my friend's house and retrieved everything from the hedges.

Drive-in theaters were so much fun. Everybody talks about the possibility of bringing them back, but it seems to be a baby boomer thing of the past.

First Love

Dating was a lot different for the baby boomer generation. There were no personal computers. That meant no instant dating site rendezvous (they had computers in the sixties, but they took up an entire room, and the information was stored on huge reel-to-reel tapes).

You met girls at school, work, or from a friend of a friend. Sometimes, you risked not knowing the other person at all. Those were called blind dates. You didn't even know what the person looked like!

My grandmother told me about pie socials her generation had. Girls would bake a pie, and guys would bid on them at an auction. If you had the highest bid, you got to sit down, meet the girl, and have a slice of pie. That sounded perfect for me, but I was one generation too late.

My first recollection of attempts to connect with a fair maiden occurred in second grade. I guess she was in my class or at least my school. She lived about half a mile from my house. I don't remember how I knew where she lived. One day, I decided to just walk by her house. On the way to her house, I noticed flowers growing in people's yards. I thought, *Why not pick a bouquet for her?* By the time I reached her house, I had quite a collection. I did not have the courage to give them to her in person. I simply rang the doorbell, placed the flowers in front of the door, and ran home. I remember having a warm feeling, just thinking about her coming to the front door and discovering the flowers. I remained anonymous until the writing of this book.

Three years later, I was in fifth grade and had another great idea for meeting girls. I was ten, and my sister was thirteen. She had a jewelry box full of nice things any girl would want. I decided to take a ring from the box and give it to a pretty girl. I ran the plan past by my closest friend. He thought it was a great idea. We decided to just put the ring inside a girl's classroom desk. He leaked the plan to other students in the school. Soon, it became common knowledge. Freddy Barnette was going to give some girl a ring in school. This became a daily nightmare for me. Every day, students would ask me which girl received the ring. Girls were constantly searching through their desks every morning to see if they were the recipient. I had to get this over with so I could go back to a normal life. I decided a girl in sixth grade would receive the ring. Her name was Gail, and her classroom was right across the hall. I thought Gail was the prettiest girl in the school, even though she was a year older.

The big moment finally arrived. My friend snuck into the classroom and put the ring on Gail's desk. I thought my troubles were over. Later that day, there was a knock on our classroom door. My teacher opened the door, and there was Gail with her teacher. Her teacher asked, "May we see Freddy Barnette in the hall?"

I went out there, thinking I was in big trouble. The teacher told me we needed to talk. He directed me to the library down the hall. When we got to the library, the teacher said, "I think Gail has something to say to you."

Gail put her hand out with the ring resting on her palm. She said, "Freddy, I can't accept this ring because I'm in sixth grade and you're only in fifth."

I really didn't care, I just wanted this to finally end. I snuck the ring back into my sister's jewelry box and breathed a sigh of relief. Sixty years later, I noticed Gail on Facebook. She lives right up the street from me in the same town. I asked her if she remembered the ring incident. She doesn't! How can that be? I remember it like it was yesterday. Oh well, it was over sixty years ago.

Fifth and sixth grade

In high school, a girl asked me to take her to homecoming. I was good friends with her brother. She went to an all-girls private Catholic high school. She was a nice girl and attractive, so I decided to go. However, I didn't know anybody and felt out of place. There was a dance and a party afterward. I don't know why I didn't ask to see her again. I suppose I just wanted to return to events at my school.

Then there were the girls from Colesville, Maryland. I went to the Montgomery County Fair with my friends, Charlie and Fred. We went to the carnival section. We passed a horse racing game. People sat down in front of a little pinball machine and pulled a lever as fast as they could. A metal ball would run through the pinball machine and eventually return to the lever. There was a large screen in front of the players. You could watch the progress of your horse until a bell rang, signaling the end of the race. Somebody had to win each race. We noticed four cute girls playing the game. We started talking to them, and, eventually, they gave us their phone numbers. The girls lived in Colesville, Maryland, and attended Springbrook High School. That would be about a forty-five-minute car trip to see them. Fred and I were sixteen and had a driver's license. Charlie was only fifteen.

We went to Colesville several times, but the girls were not allowed to date. One time, a girl named Jenny told me she could sneak out of the house if I came down. One night, I went to her house and sure enough, she came out of the house and met me in her backyard. There were lots of overgrown bushes, so we sat down behind them and started kissing. After about fifteen minutes, her mother came out on the porch and began calling her name. She had to go back into the house. We attempted to see the girls a few more times. We eventually lost interest and just gave up. I would meet up with Jenny about two years later at a party. It did not go well. I'll elaborate more later in this book. Even now, years later, I see Charlie from time to time. He'll say, "Hey, Fred, can I get a ride to Colesville?"

I liked a girl in my neighborhood named Georgia. She liked to be called Jo. She was the girl that rode around the neighborhood while we were playing street football. In junior high, I would just watch her house from a nearby forest. I was just hoping to catch a glimpse of her. My family had a boat docked on the Potomac River. I guess I asked her to go along one day. I remember seeing her swimming around the boat in her bathing suit. She was gorgeous. In eleventh grade, I asked her to go to a school dance. She was very quiet during the dance. It seemed kind of awkward. However, when we got back to her house, she was very affectionate. I was going to ask her out again, but I met someone else that blew me away. After college, about six years later, Georgia got married at her house. I was single at the time with no girlfriend. I saw all the parked cars at her house and thought that could have been me.

I had the same problem most guys had during their adolescence. We all wanted to date one of the top ten girls in the school. Those girls were never available because they always had boyfriends. I met lots of nice girls during my school days. I was way too picky.

It was the summer of 1967, before the start of my senior year in high school. I was working as an usher at a movie theater. We learned that a second concession girl would soon be hired. I was hoping for a cute girl that I could possibly ask out. One day, I got the official news that Pam would be the new girl. I was so disappointed. She was clearly out of my league. Pam was a cheerleader and would later be voted the most popular girl in the senior class. Why couldn't they have hired a regular girl that someone had a chance with?

Pam started working at the theater, and I found her easy to talk to. Her boyfriend recently broke up with her and moved to North Carolina. I knew him from the school band. I was in his brother's band, the "Reverbs," out of Damascus. She was down in the dumps after the breakup. I guess I was a shoulder to cry on.

We had a projectionist named Danny who took a liking to Pam. People noticed his attraction to her. Other employees decided to play a practical joke on Danny. They told Danny that Pam really liked him and was hoping that they could start dating. Poor Danny took the bait and asked her out. I really never heard any particulars, but somehow, she said, "No thanks."

Next, they started in on me. "Pam really likes you and was hoping you would ask her out." I wasn't going to make a fool out of myself, so I just remained casual with her. Kathy, the other concession stand girl, approached me later and said that Pam really liked me. I found it hard to believe, but I didn't think Kathy would lead me on. It was just too hard to believe she would be interested in me. I wasn't that popular, didn't play football, and was only average-looking. The next night at the theater, I was cleaning up after a birthday party. The party was held in a separate room. Pam entered the room and started helping me clean up. I could tell she was very nervous and quiet. Why was she even there? Finally, she said, "Fred, I have something to tell you."

I remembered what Kathy had told me and thought it must be true. I said, "You really like me?"

She simply said, "Yes."

I woke up that day and was just a regular guy, going to my movie theater job. Now I'm going to date the most popular girl in our senior class!

That night, we decided to drive down to the Rockville Volunteer Fire Department carnival on my motorcycle. We were standing on the midway, in front of some sideshow. Pam suddenly turned around and kissed me. We kissed some more in the parking lot before putting our helmets on. We drove to her house and said our goodbyes. I remember driving to my house feeling like I was floating in the air. This was just too good to be true.

Pam and I really enjoyed the last three weeks of summer before our senior year started. We rode everywhere on the motorcycle. Her mother called it a "Yondahonda." I guess that's a half Yamaha and a half Honda motorcycle. We went to the county fair. It was a real challenge to get into the fairgrounds without paying. There was a fence around the fairgrounds, but you could easily climb over it. You had to run about a hundred yards across a field before blending into the crowd. Boy Scouts patrolled the perimeter with whistles. If they saw someone climbing the fence or running across the field, they blew their whistles. Adults would run toward the sound of the whistle and attempt to catch you. Pam and I made it with ease. I remember winning something for her. I had to throw baseballs at metal milk bottles. Kids enjoy fairs and carnivals today. They're lots of fun, and you get to see your school friends again.

One day, we decided to go to a rock quarry. Teenagers would go there to jump off rocks or just swim. It was strictly against the law to be there, but teenagers still took the chance. It is located in Dickerson, Maryland, and kids still go there. This time, we drove a car and took my fifteen-year-old brother. Pam and Jimmy were swimming around at one end of the quarry. There were several natural rock platforms you could jump from. They ranged anywhere from twenty feet above water to one hundred and fifty feet above water. I decided to impress Pam by jumping from the highest platform. You had to jump far enough out so you hit the water and not the side of the cliff. I jumped out and cleared the rest of the cliff. I had my arms straight out instead of up over my head. I did hit feetfirst. I had no trouble swimming to the surface and getting out of the water. Rumor had it that several people had died making that same jump.

Quarry

The next day, I was working as a cashier at People's Drug. They now call them CVS drugstores. Each time I reached down for a bag, I would get this pain in my side. I tried to continue working, but the pain became too intense. I told the store manager I had to leave. I was riding a motorcycle and started to have problems breathing. I made it home but collapsed in the front yard. My mother came out. I told her I couldn't breathe. She thought I was kidding at first. It was weird. I could find some positions where I was fine. If I moved to another position, I started having breathing problems again. My parents took me to the hospital emergency room. The doctor examined me and told my parents I had a collapsed lung. They cut a hole in my side and ran a tube down to my lung. Fluid from my lung drained into a jug. I was there for about three days. Pam would come with my parents for visits. I think the impact from the quarry jump caused my lung to collapse.

We went to the Chesapeake and Ohio Canal towpath. We walked along the towpath and swam in the Potomac River. Finally, it was time to go back to school. I couldn't wait to get back to school and tell everybody who I was dating.

Our senior year started, and I was so proud of my new girlfriend. She was so down-to-earth. She immediately fit into my group of friends. She ate lunch with me everyday day. It was always Fred, John, Pam, and me. The senior banquet was in September of that year. It was at a nice restaurant called the Peter Pan Inn. It was sort of a semiformal affair (it was a baby boomer experience). Senior banquets soon came to an end. In fact, our 1967 banquet was the last one Gaithersburg High School ever had. Pam and I went through the school year doing all the usual high school activities. There were football and basketball games she cheered for. There were parties at houses. Baby boomers had lots of field parties. Kids would just meet up in a field, park their cars, have a few beers, and socialize. We went to the homecoming dance and the prom. Pam and I were best friends and soulmates.

I gave her a bracelet to signify our relationship. Her name was on one side, and my name was on the other. We attended a party, and she had to go to the bathroom. There was no facility, so she decided to go into a cornfield. She discovered that the bracelet slipped off her wrist when she was in the cornfield. We never found it, and she was so upset. We went to a party in a housing development called Rosemont. My buddy came up to me and said Jenny from Colesville was there. He said that Jenny was telling people that if she saw me, she was going to slap my face. I didn't think much of it. What reason would she have to do that? Pam and I descended a few steps and entered the basement. Jenny came charging across the room, yelled, "I hate you!" and slapped my face.

I just looked at her and said, "Are you happy now?" It was embarrassing, so we left the party. I told Pam the truth about meeting Jenny in her backyard two years ago. We went back to Pam's house. Her mom asked why we weren't at the party. Pam told her we had to leave because some girl slapped my face. Pam and I finished high school and ended up at Montgomery Junior College the following year. Now they call them community colleges.

I was just too immature for a serious long-term relationship. Most guys can't handle long-term, committed relationships at seventeen. I started taking her for granted and wondering what other girls would be like. Dating became routine and kind of boring. I made every mistake in the book. Even after sixty years, I beat myself up over losing her. My friend wanted to go to Florida over the Christmas break to visit colleges. He asked me to go along. Worst mistake in my life. Christmas is such a special time to spend with someone you love. I left her at Christmas and headed to Florida with my buddy. It has put a damper on Christmas for the rest of my life. Every year, I think about the stupid mistake I made. After eighteen months of dating, I told her I wanted to be free. She didn't say much. I don't even remember what she said, but it was pretty much just okay. I didn't realize it at the time, but she already had someone to take my place. While I was in Florida, she decided to see someone else. He would visit Pam at her workplace, from time to time, and flirt with her. I knew about this but never considered it to be a threat. He had been married and had a son.

After six weeks, I decided the grass wasn't greener on the other side. I missed my best friend and soulmate. I hadn't even asked any other girl out during that time. I decided to call her and reconnect. Her mother answered the phone and said Pam had gone bowling. I drove to the bowling alley. As I was going in the bowling alley, Pam and her new boyfriend were coming out. She didn't notice me and started to walk down the sidewalk. She was laughing and just had that look of love about her. I called her name out, and she turned around. She acted surprised and asked, "Oh, hi, what are you doing here?"

I said, "I came to see you."

Pam stated that she was "going with" Norman now. He was the divorced man with a son.

That was the end for me. I tried everything to get her back, but nothing worked. Each attempt was followed by an encounter with her new boyfriend. He always threatened me with something, but nothing ever got physical. I made a sign that said I love you. I drove up to the front of the dry cleaners where she worked and held the sign up. That evening, I was working at the pharmacy at People's drugstore. Here came the new boyfriend, right up to the counter, in front of customers, the pharmacist, and the store manager.

He threatened me again with, "If you don't leave Pam alone, your ass is grass, and I'm a lawn mower!" That was really original. He then turned around and walked out of the store. I was so embarrassed. The store manager felt my humiliation and made some joke about it. How could she send that goon into my place of employment? Yes, I didn't deserve a second chance, but I didn't deserve that. Eventually, I had no choice but to try to move on.

It was a dark, lonely time for me. I contemplated suicide. I stopped attending my college classes but didn't even bother to withdraw. After my first semester, my grade point average was 0.9. I was put on academic probation and had to sit out the next semester. I got a new, higher-paying job. I delivered building materials to jobsites.

One day, I had to carry bundles of hardwood floorboards into a new house. I had to put the bundles in the various rooms. The new job was the wake-up call I needed. I never applied myself in school. My high school English teacher called me up to his desk, late in the school year. He asked me if I was going to go to college the following year. I said yes, I would be attending Montgomery Junior College in Rockville, Maryland.

He then warned me with, "Let me tell you this. If you don't study any more in college than you did in high school, you won't have a snowball's chance in hell."

I decided that this time, I was going back to college and apply myself.

I went back and really enjoyed studying and doing the assignments. Learning was a new experience for me. I earned a 3.4 and decided to transfer to a four-year college and major in education. I was going to be an elementary school teacher. One day, I was walking through the student union and noticed a rack with college catalogs displayed. There was a catalog for Salisbury State College. On the cover of the catalog, a pretty girl was walking on the beach. Salisbury State College is located thirty minutes from Ocean City, Maryland. That's the school for me! In the back of the catalog was an admission form. I filled it out and sent it in. A week later, I was notified that I was accepted. A new chapter in my life was about to begin.

I saw Pam five years after the breakup. I was working at a gas station, and her husband pulled in for gas. He got out and recognized me. We talked a little bit about nothing important. I was home for the summer from college. In 1973, you didn't pump your own gas. The gas station attendant asked you how much you wanted, and they pumped the gas. It was so strange. Pam didn't get out or even roll the window down. She just had this Mona Lisa smile as I walked past her window. Most people would have at least rolled the window down and said hello. I got the feeling that she was too afraid to acknowledge me. They drove away, and she never glanced back.

Five years later, Pam would die in a horse-riding accident. She was competing in a steeplechase race in Maryland. She was running second but gaining on the leader. Her horse hesitated at the last jump, causing Pam to fall forward over the jump. Then the horse fell over the jump and on top of her. Her obituary said she had a broken collarbone, sternum, had broken seven ribs, hip, and pelvis, a collapsed lung, and internal bleeding. She was only twenty-eight years old.

Segregation

The baby boomer generation started in 1946 and ended in 1964. The name came from the increased rate of births after World War II. Most baby boomers witnessed some form of segregation as they were growing up. You didn't have to live in the Deep South. I was born in 1950. As a young boy, I had no knowledge of what segregation was. Two examples stood out in my mind as I reached adulthood. We had to ride our bikes about four miles to get candy or soda pop. The establishment was called Snuffy's Tavern. It was a combination liquor store and restaurant. The liquor store was attached to the restaurant. We always went to the carryout side for our candy or soda pop. On the front door of the restaurant was a big sign that said White Only. I thought the sign meant you could only get white bread at the restaurant. They didn't serve rye, whole wheat, or any other kind of bread. I realized later that White Only meant Blacks could use the carryout but would not be served in the restaurant.

Snuffy's Tavern

There was an amusement park in Cabin John, Maryland, that also had a large, Olympic-style pool. The park was called Glenn Echo Park. I went there with my family several times. Black people started picketing the park during the summer of 1960. They stood in front of Glenn Echo every day, holding signs. Blacks were not allowed in the park or pool. The Civil Rights Act of 1964 was passed prohibiting segregation of public establishments. Blacks were finally permitted to enter the park. However, White people stopped going for the most part. The park closed in 1968. I suppose it just wasn't doing enough business.

Civil rights were a huge movement during the sixties. We also saw several assassinations during this time period. President John F. Kennedy was shot and killed in 1963. He was riding in an open car during a parade in Dallas, Texas. His brother, Robert, ran for president in 1968. Robert Kennedy had just made a speech after winning the California primary. The Secret Service officers decided to take a shortcut through the kitchen to avoid the crowds. He was shot and killed in the kitchen. Martin Luther King, the Black Civil Rights leader, was shot and killed on a Memphis, Tennessee, hotel balcony in 1968.

Vietnam

Baby boomers experienced two wars. I don't remember anything about the Korean War. The United States was involved with the Korean War from 1950 until 1955. I was much too young to remember anything. It ended when I was five. Vietnam was another story. We sent military advisers to Vietnam in 1961. In 1965, we started sending actual combat troops. During this time, there was a military draft system in place. When a young man turned eighteen, he had to go to a draft office and register for the draft. It was against the law not to register. You received a draft card proving you had registered. Young men who turned eighteen could be drafted and end up in Vietnam. However, they had deferments that exempted you from military duty. College students had such a deferment. From 1965 to 1969, college students had nothing to worry about. The war became very unpopular, and people started questioning the college deferment. Poor men were being drafted, and rich kids were protesting the war in college, out of harm's way.

The government came up with a lottery system in 1969. Now, the war affected me. I was nineteen, and college students no longer had a deferment. They placed all the days of the year in a hat and pulled out one at a time. My birthday was April 28, and it was pulled out as number 264. People who had a number over two hundred were safe. I was taking a class called elementary swimming and diving at the junior college. I walked into the locker room to change for the pool. All the guys in the locker room were crowded around a newspaper. I thought they must be looking at sports scores. I asked, "What's everybody looking at?"

One student replied, "Didn't you hear? The lottery numbers came out."

My 264 number was safe, but one of my friends got number 2. Mike quit school that day and joined the National Guard. The war lasted another four years. There is no longer a draft system. The United States of America now has an all-volunteer armed forces plan.

The Remarkable Find

I retired in 2004 from the Frederick County, Maryland, public school system. I had a thirty-year career as a fourth-grade classroom teacher, elementary library media specialist, middle school library media specialist, and middle school assistant principal. A church group was going on a mission trip to Mississippi and needed a drummer for their praise band. I offered to join them. I was retired now, and this would be my first trip.

When I got back from the mission trip, my wife informed me that she had received a strange phone call. The conversation went something like this:

"Hello, may I speak to Fred Barnette?"

"I'm sorry. He's not home."

"Did he go to Gaithersburg High School?"

"Yes."

"Did he graduate in 1968?"

"Yes."

"I found his class ring in my flower bed. Here is my number. Have him call me."

In 1967, I lost my class ring playing baseball in a farmer's field. The ring was a little loose, and in the process of putting on and taking a baseball glove off, it slipped off my finger. We searched for about thirty minutes but eventually gave up. Now, thirty-five years later, this kind lady had found it.

I called her. She explained that she had a landscaped flower bed. She was planting bulbs in it and struck something. It didn't sound like a rock, so she dug a little deeper. There in a spade full of dirt was my ring. She cleaned it off and noticed the name of the high school, the class date, and my initials inside. She drove to Gaithersburg High School, about thirty minutes away. She entered the building and went to the front office. She explained to the secretaries what she had discovered. "Do you have any old yearbooks?" she asked.

"We have some old yearbooks. What year do you need?" The lady said *1968*, and the secretaries said, "Oh, I don't know if we go back that far." I was the only senior in the yearbook with the initials FWB. I don't know how she found my phone number in a different county.

I asked what kind of shape the ring was in after being underground for thirty-five years. She said it was in perfect condition. I'm looking at the ring right now. It has a smooth blue stone. Encircling the stone are the words *Gaithersburg High School*. One side has a Trojan head with the word *Trojans* underneath; 68 is written in numbers above the Trojan head. The other side has 19 written in numbers. The great seal of Maryland is below the number. Below the seal is the school motto "Knowledge Is Power." It really is in perfect condition and quite beautiful. I wear it occasionally, especially on karaoke nights.

I drove to her house and met the lady and her ten-year-old daughter. She wanted to know if I had become a policeman. In the yearbook, policeman was listed as my ambition. I informed her that I had become an elementary school teacher. The ring was about three hundred yards from the makeshift baseball field. The field had become a housing development. Bulldozers had pushed the ring to a new location. What do you give someone who went through all that effort to reconnect you with your class ring? I went to a nursery and purchased a rosebush. She planted it in the exact location where she found the ring. When I tell this story, people always say a few things. I often hear, "You should write that story up and send it to *Readers Digest*." People also say, "I don't know what's more amazing. The actual find or the effort that lady went through to find you." I wish I had written her name down. It would be nice to send her a Christmas card every year. Maybe I'll get lucky, and this book will be published. Perhaps she'll read it. That's not any more amazing than finding a class ring buried in your flower bed for thirty-five years!

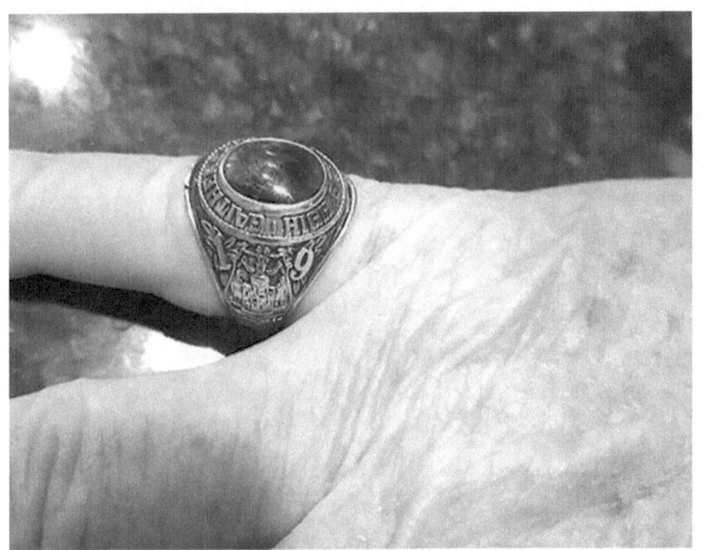

1968 class ring

Gone but Not Forgotten

Baby boomers, like any generation, have seen some major changes in our lifetime. I would like to mention just three. There were no plastic trash bags in the fifties. I'll never forget the trashman visiting my house one morning. I was about six years old. The year was 1956. In those days, people just put their trash in a large, galvanized trash can with a matching lid. That day, the trashman laid a large burlap tarp on the ground. He picked the trash can up and dumped the garbage out in the middle of the tarp. He picked the tarp up by its four edges and slung it over his back. He looked like Santa Claus carrying a sack of toys to the sled, only this was garbage. As he was walking, liquids would be dripping out of the bottom. Today, all garbage is placed in plastic bags and put in a portable dumpster that you push to the edge of the road. A garbage truck comes by and stops at the dumpster. A large arm, attached to the truck, grabs hold of the dumpster, lifts it in the air, and the trash descends into the truck. Later that day, the patron wheels the dumpster back to the house. Plastic garbage can liners are a godsend.

I recall sitting on the front stoop of our modest home in Rockville, Maryland, with my father. He was so excited about an invention. My dad loved listening to big band swing music. He played trumpet in dance bands for years. In the early fifties, people listened to LP 33 rpm records on phonographs. There was one speaker in the phonograph. My dad started describing something called stereo high-fidelity sound systems. The record player had two speakers attached to it. Bass came out of one speaker, and the melody came out of the other speaker. He said it was like sitting right in front of the orchestra.

Stoop where my dad told me about stereo high-fidelity sound

Baby boomers have experienced dramatic changes in televisions also. Television was developed throughout the fifties. In 1950, only 9 percent of American families had a television in their home. Only black-and-white television sets were available. Color television became available in 1954. However, only a few shows were in color. The television was small at first. There was no cable or satellite dish. An antenna was placed on top of the television. It consisted of two metal rods that could be moved back and forth to improve reception. It was nicknamed rabbit ears. You could only get four local television stations. There were no solid-state televisions in the fifties. Televisions had tubes inside that had to be replaced from time to time, like a light bulb. I remember the television repairman coming to our house with a big satchel in his hand. He would open the satchel displaying various sizes of tubes. Drugstores had tube-testing machines. People brought their tubes to the store to see if they were good or burned out. There were no remote controls for early televisions. You had to get up off the couch and change stations or volume on the set itself.

Baby boomers have also seen the disappearance of pay phones, cash registers, typewriters, drugstore lunch counters, video stores, and roller-skating rinks. Life moves on. You must get with it or get left behind.

Montgomery Ward was a very popular department store for the baby boomer generation. In fact, I worked at the store in 1974. I worked on the loading dock, helping people who purchased big items. It was fun tying a couch on top of a Volkswagen. The stores were founded in 1872 and went bankrupt in 1997. They just couldn't compete with Target and Walmart.

I made an interesting purchase in 1969. I was just walking around the store with my girlfriend at the time. If a store has a pet section, I always visit it. Usually, you see fish, hamsters, and para-keets. But that day, I saw several monkeys. I believe they were squirrel monkeys. I envisioned this cute little monkey sitting on my shoulder or walking around with me on a leash, entertaining people. There was one problem: they cost fifty dollars. I borrowed the money from my girlfriend and made the purchase.

When I got home, I let the monkey out of the cardboard box. He was not this cute little fellow that would sit on your shoulder. The monkey was very aggressive and would bite you if you tried to touch it. I had no cage for him. I decided to call him Moses. My closet became his new home. I removed all the clothes and tied a rope to the bar. At the other end of the rope, I tied a boxing punching bag. Moses sat on the top shelf. Perhaps, in time, Moses would calm down and become this cute little companion.

His stay was short-lived. My brother told my father I had a monkey in my bedroom. My father thought for sure he was kid-ding. He got a big surprise when he opened the closet door and saw a squirrel monkey. He boxed the monkey up and returned it to Montgomery Ward. He threatened a lawsuit if they didn't take the monkey back.

Help, I Need Tech Support

Most baby boomers are struggling with the new information technology age. Some have no problem making the transition. Others are scared to death of computers and avoid them at all costs. I suppose I'm somewhere in the middle. I love the television commercial depicting a millennial couple visiting their baby boomer parents. The parents see the couple pull up in the driveway. As they come up to the porch, the parents come to them with a trayful of devices and declare, "None of these things work."

I started writing this book with paper and pencil. The need for a computer, spellchecker, and keyboard were apparent. The same can be said about cell phones. When cell phones first came out, I was determined not to get one. Who needs another bill? Society forced me into purchasing one. Businesses and medical institutions force you to use email. Everyone wants to know your email address. My millennial son set me up with an account. Now, if I could only remember those damn passwords.

Gradually, I have learned a few computer sites. I think they're called apps. I do text friends and businesses. My DJ business required me to learn how to use Spotify. My cell phone connected to the DJ system. I could download any song in a minute using Spotify. Facebook is fun to use. I stay connected to new friends and reconnect with old ones. That's about it for me. I tell people I'm technology-challenged.

I stay in the dark ages for most other activities. I never buy anything online. Today, there seems to be only two stores. The stores would be Walmart and "I bought it online." Don't people see stores and malls closing all around them? Here's an example of a baby boomer and a millennial mindset regarding purchasing an item. I saw the movie *Remember the Titans* and wanted to get a T-shirt from the high school in the movie. The movie is about a 1971 Virginia high school that integrated their student body. The football team, therefore, was integrated for the first time. In the movie, Denzel Washington plays the head football coach. The name of the school at the time was T. C. Williams High School. I told my family I wanted to drive to Arlington, Virginia, and find the school. I wanted to ask the school if they sold T. C. Williams football T-shirts. That's what a baby boomer would plan on doing. My millennial son laughed and said, "Dad, you don't have to drive to Arlington, Virginia, to buy a T-shirt. I can go online and get you one." In ten minutes, my T-shirt was on the way.

I was wearing that T-shirt at an IHOP in Virginia. I was in line, paying my check, when a man approached me and asked if I went to T. C. Williams High School. I told him, "No. I just like the movie *Remember the Titans*." He told me he was the head football coach at T. C. Williams now. What a small world.

I never buy anything online, and I don't pay any of my bills online. I visit the actual brick-and-mortar store to purchase an item. Bills are paid with an old-fashioned check, envelope, and stamp. My father belonged to the Greatest Generation and was a World War II veteran. I could not get him to use an ATM machine.

Yes, the world is constantly changing, and I'm trying to keep up. Imagine getting a college degree online and missing campus life.

I hope you enjoyed reading about the baby boomer generation and the good old days. At least I'm retired now and have time to share my adventures. Be patient with the baby boomers. We're trying to adapt to such a fast-paced lifestyle.

The Disastrous Paint Job

Baby boomers always had some type of job growing up. I think you could get a work permit at the age of sixteen. However, many of us had jobs before that age. I worked for a farmer, and I delivered newspapers.

After turning sixteen, I held numerous jobs. The list would include bus boy, movie theater usher, dishwasher, cashier, pharmacy aide, custodian, and gas station attendant.

When I was nineteen, I worked for an industrial cleaning service. One day, the owner came to the building and held a meeting. He stated that he needed the exterior of his house painted. He would keep track of the hours and add them to your regular paycheck. That would be much cheaper than paying a professional painter. I thought some extra money would be great, so I volunteered.

I arrived at his house and decided to start with the peak of the house. I placed an extension ladder on top of the garage. I reached the peak, but the ladder shifted, and then the gallon of paint crashed down onto the garage. The paint ran down the garage shingles and into the gutter. I just stood there and watched in horror. Things got worse. The paint traveled along the gutter and ran into the downspout. The paint came out of the downspout and ran down the paved driveway.

I assessed the damage. The garage shingles were ruined, as was the paved driveway. Now what do I do? I decided to just pack up everything and go home. I never went back to work, and the owner never called me.

In a twist of irony, years later, I spent a summer painting school buildings. (I was a fourth-grade teacher and had summers off.) The school board painters had a foreman who taught you everything you needed to know about painting. I decided to start my own painting business after one summer of painting with them. I had a successful painting business for ten years before I got promoted to assistant principal at a middle school and started working for the school system in the summers.

About the Author

Fred Barnette is a retired public school educator. He was a classroom fourth-grade teacher, library media specialist, and middle school assistant principal. Today, he enjoys working in the yard, golfing, riding his motorcycle, and singing karaoke. Fred lives in Maryland with his wife, two cats (Sweetie and Whiskers), and Fluffy the rabbit.